PRODUCTION

MANAGEMENT

:: Author ::

GANESHBHAI C. NARBHAVAR

(M.COM., B.ED., G-SET)

PUBLISHED BY

Chakravarti Siddharaj Jaysinh International
Publishing House
HQ. At & Po. Chaveli., Ta- Chansma,
Dist- Patan, North Gujarat, India, Asia.
www.iphouseindia.com

PRODUCTION MANAGEMENT

First Publication: 19TH DECEMBER, 2014

Copyright: Author
(c) GANESHBHAI C. NARBHAVAR

ISBN:- 978-15-08675-62-4

Price: Rs.750/- INDIA
      $ 15 OUTSIDE INDIA

PUBLISHED BY

Chakravarti Siddharaj Jaysinh International Publishing House
HQ. At & Po. Chaveli., Ta- Chansma,
Dist- Patan, North Gujarat, India, Asia.
www.iphouseindia.com

Dedicated to my Parents

Overview of Contents

- **Understanding Production and Operations Management**

- **International Production and Operations Management (IPOM)**

- **Value Analysis: An Applied Concept for Manufacturing and Service Industry**

- **Process Design and Analysis**

- **Facility Layout - Objectives, Design and Factors Affecting the Layout**

- **Forecasting**

- **What is Aggregate Planning ? - Importance and its Strategies**

- **Operations Scheduling and Workplace Planning**

- **Inventory Management and Just In Time (JIT)**

- **Warehouse and Materials Management**

- **Material Handling - Principles, Operations and Equipment**

- **Maintenance Management**

- **Quality - A Tool for Achieving Excellence**

- **Quality Definitions**

- **World Class Manufacturing**

Understanding Production and Operations Management

Introduction

The very essence of any business is to cater needs of customer by providing services and goods, and in process create value for customers and solve their problems. Production and operations management talks about applying business organization and management concepts in creation of goods and services.

Production

Production is a scientific process which involves transformation of raw material (input) into desired product or service (output) by adding economic value. Production can broadly categorize into following based on technique:

Production through separation: It involves desired output is achieved through separation or extraction from raw materials. A classic example of separation or extraction is Oil into various fuel products.

Production by modification or improvement: It involves change in chemical and mechanical parameters of the raw material without altering physical attributes of the raw material. Annealing process (heating at high temperatures and then cooling), is example of production by modification or improvement.

Production by assembly: Car production and computer are example of production by assembly.

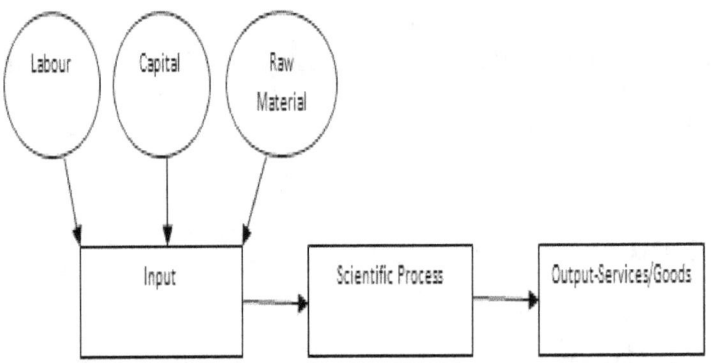

Importance of Production Function and Production Management

Successful organizations have well defined and efficient line function and support function. Production comes under the category of line function which directly affects customer experience and there by future of organization itself.

Aim of production function is to add value to product or service which will create a strong and long lasting customer relationship or association. And this can be achieved by healthy and productive association between Marketing and Production people. Marketing function people are frontline representative of the company and provide insights to real product needs of customers.

An effective planning and control on production parameters to achieve or create value for customers is called production management.

Operations Management

As to deliver value for customers in products and services, it is essential for the company to do the following:

1. Identify the customer needs and convert that into a specific product or service (numbers of products required for specific period of time)
2. Based on product requirement do back-ward working to identify raw material requirements
3. Engage internal and external vendors to create supply chain for raw material and finished goods between vendor → production facility → customers.

Operations management captures above identified 3 points.

Production Management v/s Operations Management

A high level comparison which distinct production and operations management can be done on following characteristics:

- **Output:** Production management deals with manufacturing of products like (computer, car, etc) while operations management cover both products and services.

- **Usage of Output:** Products like computer/car are utilized over a period of time whereas services need to be consumed immediately

- **Classification of work:** To produce products like computer/car more of capital equipment and less labour are required while services require more labour and lesser capital equipment.

- **Customer Contact:** There is no participation of customer during production whereas for services a constant contact with customer is required.

Operations: Policy and Strategy

Introduction

It is very important for an organization to have well defined objective. A well-defined objective facilitates development of strategies and policy thereby creating value for customers.

Operation Strategy

Operational strategy is essential to achieve operational goals set by organization in alignment with overall objective of the company. Operational strategy is design to achieve business effectiveness or competitive advantage.

Operational strategy is planning process which aligns the following:

In this global competitive age organization goal tend to change from time to time therefore operations strategy as a consequence has also be dynamic in nature. A regular SWOT analysis ensures that the organization is able to maintain competitive advantage and business leadership.

Strategic Management Process for Production and Operation

For success of organizational strategic objective, strategic planning has to trickle down to various function areas of the business. In order to build strategy management process a sequential process as below is followed

Competition Analysis: In this step company evaluates and studies current competition in the market and practices that are followed in the industry for operations and production vis-à-vis company policies

Goal Setting: Next step involves narrowing down the objective towards which the organization wants to move towards.

Strategy Formulation: The next step is breaking down of organizational goals into operations and production strategies.

Implementation: The final step is to convert operations and production strategies into day to day activities like production schedule, product design, quality management etc.

As organizations are always customer-centric, production and operation strategy for organization are built around them

Productivity

Measurement of formulated operations and production strategy is important to maintain alignment with the organization objectives. In simple terms productivity is defined as sum of total output per employee or per day. Productivity of company is dependent on industry and environmental conditions in which it is operating.

Two essential part of productivity are labor and capital. In scenario of limited resources, optimum and efficient utilization of labor and capital will generate favorable productivity. Productivity measurement also enables company to identify areas which require improvement or special focus. Also productivity provides ready report card to measure status against company's production objective.

Productivity measurement can be classified in three categories based on the inputs used for calculation. Partial productivity ration of output is compared to one of resource used for example, labor productivity where output is compared to the labor wages.

Total productivity measure takes into consideration sum of all input factors which are used for the output.

In the modern age technology plays an important part in productivity.

Wastivity

Another important factor is the case of production is wastivity. Not 100% of input would be converted to output, there is going to waste during production. Wastivity is reciprocal of productivity. Classic examples of wastivity are defective products and services which either have to be re-cycle or disposed of completely. Other example is idle capacity of material, man-power equipment etc.

International Production and Operations Management (IPOM)

Introduction

International production and operations management deals with production of goods and services in international locations and markets. It involves management process which has to take into consideration local production market (labor and capital) and international customer requirements.

Nature of IPOM

The foundation for international production and operations is no different to domestic production and operations management. But there are certain aspects which make international exposure a challenge for an organization. The very 1st difference is international business environment where not just economics but also international quality standards have to be maintained. The 2nd aspect is the international stint makes the company more aware of its surroundings thus making it more competitive.

As IPOM is dynamic in nature, organization has to design it strategic objectives which cover following points:

- Meeting international quality standards
- Forecasting demand and production design
- Profitability
- Minimum production cost
- Adaptation to modern available technology

Domestic POM and IPOM

Organization has to clearly identify challenges it is likely to face in an international environment. Those challenges can be categorized as follows:

Culture: Domestic POM has to content with homogenous culture where as IPOM has to content with multi-culture multi-ethnicity scenario.

Business Environment: Domestic POM has to consider local economical and social factors where as IPOM has to deal with economical and social factors across geography and countries.

Quality Standards: Domestic POM has to look at single local market therefore not much variation in quality standards where as IPOM has to consider different international markets with different quality standard requirements.

Pricing: Pricing for Domestic POM may not be a challenge as competition would also operate in the same environment. IPOM has to consider the customer paying capacity which may vary from developed country to developing country.

Technology: In domestic environment innovation and usage of technology is much more comparable among competition. For IPOM owing to different quality and pricing requirements investment in technology becomes important.

Economies of Scale: Domestic POM has to deal with limited local market, hence limiting scope of economies of scale whereas IPOM has to access to larger market thus providing a change of achieving larger economies of scale.

Market Segmentation: Domestic POM is around local market where as IPOM has to developed and diversified market.

Usage of resources: Domestic POM has to deal with in-flexibility of moving around of resources within one location while IPOM has advantage of moving around of resources from high cost market to low cost market.

IPOM Strategies

Organization needs to consider the following point while developing IPOM strategies:

Production/Factory Location: The choice of location for the production facility depends on its proximity near to the market and cost of production (labor) in that particular environment.

Factory design, layout and quality standards: Organization need to standardize design and layout across their production location as to minimize production planning process, provide flexibility in sharing technical knowledge and manpower.

External vendor and procurement: Organization needs to finalize the vendors to provide raw material as well important components required to complete the final product. Also procurement schedule has to be finalized as not to hurt production.

Managing Technology in Operations Management

Introduction

In last decade or so technology has changed the way organization conduct their business. Advent of technology in operation management has increased productivity of the organization.

Technology and Operations Management

The scope of Technology and operation management has evolved over a period of time and has moved from development of products into design, management and improvement of operating system and processes.

Usage of technology in operation management has ensured that organizations are able to reduce the cost, improve the delivery process, standardize and improve quality and focus on customization, thereby creating value for customers.

Integration of Technology with Production System

Technology drives efficiency in organization and increases' productivity of the organization. However, bringing technology in the production system is highly complex process, and it needs to following steps:

Technology Acquisition: technology acquired should align with overall objectives of the organization and should be approved after elaborate cost-benefit analysis.

Technology Integration: technology affects all aspects of production i.e. capital, labour and customer. Therefore, a solid technology integration plan is required.

Technology Verification: once technology integrated, it is important to check whether technology is delivering operational effectiveness and is been used to its fullest.

Technology in Manufacturing and Design

Technology is getting extensively used in customization of design products and services. The usage of computers and supporting electronic systems is integral part of modern industrial and services industry. Current techniques can be broadly classified into following categories:

Computer-Aided Design (CAD): CAD facilitates linking of two more complex components of design at very high level of accuracy thus delivering higher productivity.

Computer-Aided Manufacturing System (CAM): Precision is very essential in operating any machines and therefore, Computerized Numerically Controlled machines are used, thus ensuring highest level of accuracy.

Standard for the Exchange of Product Data: As the name suggests product design is transmitted among CAM and CAM in three dimensions. Standard for The Exchange of Product Data process sharing of product across all phases of product life cycle and serves as neutral file exchange.

Software Systems in Manufacturing

There are various software systems available to integrated operations and manufacturing functions with other business functions of organization. Some of the common software systems are Enterprise Resource Planning (ERP), Supply-Chain Management (SCM), New-Product Development (NPD) and Customer Relationship Management (CRM).

Enterprises Resources Planning (ERP) links all business functions like manufacturing, marketing, human resource and finance through a common software platform. The main benefits of the ERP solution are that it not only reduces database errors but also delivers value to customer through faster delivery and order fulfillment.

Automation in Production and Operations

Automation reduces manual intervention in the manufacturing process. It increases productivity and reduces margin of error thereby facilitating economies of scale. There is this-advantages of automation also, such as unemployment, high breakdown cost and initial capital investment. Therefore, automation may not be suitable in all situations and in the end alignment with an overall organization objective is important.

Challenges

Technology can be facilitating factor in bringing about change in operations and production management. But it may not be feasible to use technology in all aspects with challenge coming through high initial cost of investment, high cost of maintenance and mismanagement.

Value Analysis: An Applied Concept for Manufacturing and Service Industry

Introduction

All organizations strive to create value for their customers. This value creates mind space for product and services. Value analysis, therefore, is a scientific method to increase this value.

Value is a perception hence every customer will have their own perceptions on how they define value. However, overall at the highest level, value is quality, performance, style, design relative to product cost. Increasing value necessarily does not mean decrease in all-inclusive cost of production but providing something extra for which a premium can be charged.

The objective and benefits of value analysis can be summarized as below:

- Value analysis aims to simplify products and process. There by increasing efficiency in managing projects, resolve problems, encourage innovation and improve communication across organization.

- Value analysis enables people to contribute in the value addition process by continuous focus on product design and services.

- Value analysis provides a structure through cost saving initiatives, risk reduction and continuous improvement.

Activities for Value Analysis

Activities for value analysis are separated into following activities:

Product/Service - The 1st step is to identify the product or service which is based on usage/demand, complexity in development and future potential.

Cost Analysis: The next step understands in detail cost structure in developing and manufacturing the product.

Define product and function: The next step is to define all the primary function of the product and service through satisfying the basic need and then taking next step in delighting the customer. For this better understanding of product components and characteristics is required.

Evaluation of alternatives: Through brainstorming possible alternatives can short listed which can provide value to the primary function of the product. Cost evaluation at high level needs to be done for all the alternatives, and the cheapest alternative is short listed.

Secondary Function evaluation: Secondary functions of the product and services are studied and evaluated.

Recommendation: Value Analysis done has to communicate to the various level of the management team as to get acceptance.

Value Analysis Team

The process of value analysis is carried out by value analysis team. So it becomes paramount that team selection for value analysis also follows a structured process. Value analysis team consists of trained and qualified team members who have background and knowledge about the project. Team leader is selected by the project manager. Team size for value analysis is 5 to 8.

Value Analysis Process

Value analysis process can be divided into three phases of mainly pre-analysis, analysis and post analysis. Pre-analysis contains activities of project selection and team selection. Analysis phase as the name suggests consists of activities like investigation, speculation, evaluation, development and presentation of the report. Post analysis consists of activities' implementation of the report and regular audit.

Functional Analysis part of Value Analysis

Function analysis is required to transform the project elements from design of product towards function of product. The main categories are Basic, Secondary, Required Secondary Aesthetic, Unwanted, Higher Order and Assumed.

Effective Product Design

Introduction

Organization success is dependent on customer satisfaction and delight. Customer satisfaction is achieved through development of product and service, which have all attributes required by the customer. A success product or services do not only have attractive package design but should be also able to provide robust performance.

Thus, product design must be practical enough for production and powerful enough to provide a competitive advantage.

Product Design

A good product design has following common features:

- **Utility:** The product design should make product utility as per expectation of customers and provide steady performance through the product life.
- **Aesthetics:** Product aesthetics is important in success of the product. The product aesthetics is dependent on market and end customer.
- **Producible:** Product design should enable effective production of product through available production methods.
- **Profitability:** Product design should make economic sense as to deliver value to customer and sustainability to the organization.
- **Differentiable:**A good product design should enable product to be differentiate among its competition. This

can be achieved by attractive packaging and also by providing additional service on the product.

Objectives of Product Design

The essence of product design is to satisfy customer and maximizes the value for the customer at minimum cost. The product or service should also be able to meet primary needs and desire of the customer. This may not require development of new product, but enhancement to existing product or service.

Stages of Product Design

Product design is a creative process which looks at all the available options and beyond. The process is can be divided into three stages:

1. **First stage:** His stage involves brainstorming, bringing ideas and analysis of customer and market feedback.
2. **Second Stage:** Idea is converted into a feasible solution to satisfy the customer expectation, using available resource and technology.
3. **Third Stage:** This is the last stage in which the product is introduced in the market.

Factors Affecting Product Design

A successful product design is combination factors as follows:

Correct Team Selection: This is very essential to get the correct team in place which has expert designers who are not only aware and comfortable with technology but also understanding of customer expectation.

Customer Involvement: Involvement of customer in product design and testing can provide insight into the direction of the project

Prototyping and testing: Product design is high risk concept as it involves commitment of capital and man-power; therefore, it is imperative that extensive prototyping and testing are done with customer and market.

Raw Material: It is essential that raw material to be used in the production meets the quality standards of the end product. Furthermore, procurement system needs to be in place to ensure continuous, cost effective supply.

Production method and process layout: Feasibility of production method and process layout determines future success of the product.

External Factors: Environmental and government regulations plays an important part in product design. And these norms are updated from time to time, so product design should have the flexibility to adapt.

Product Selection

Production selection process is done through a combination of financial analysis, risk analysis, existing product portfolio, raw material supply and pre-determined product criteria.

Process Design and Analysis

Introduction

The objective of organization is to provide service and product, which satisfy customer and create value for them. A product and service designed is based on the customer feedback and requirement of the market. Process design is where the product is broken down into parts, which further can be helpful in the actual manufacturing process.

A product, for example, has attractive packaging to provide the right aesthetics plus has function and features, which provide value to customers. Process design ensures that there is smooth and continuous relationship between required output and all the intermediate process.

For example, manufacturing of Air-Conditioners, process design has to be such that maximum supply is achieved during the hot months of summer when demand of the product is at the highest. So people, process and machines need to align to give continuous production throughout the year as to satisfy seasonal demand.

Process Planning

Process development for process design can be summarized through following steps:

1. **Process Requirement:** The very 1st step is to collect and gather information to give structure with the end objective. That is to make process requirement document highlighting various stages, risk and stakeholders for production. This will include assessment of available technology, raw material requirement, factory/plant layout and demand forecast.

2. **Team Building:** Once the process requirements are finalized, for each objective, a team is finalized based on skill level and experience. Function of the team is to get familiarize with the whole process.

3. **Planning and Implementation:** Process planning team will develop module; policies and procedure require for production, which are after required approval internal as well as external is implemented.

4. **Audit:** A regular audit is carried out to ensure that process thus implemented is in line and delivering value to customers.

5. **End of Life:** Over a course of time there may be enhancement of the product or product may get

discontinued in these circumstances, process thus develop is discontinued.

Production Process

Based on the nature of product and service production or conversion process can be divided into two broad categories, continuous production (assembly line, oil refinery) and intermittent production (job work, service).

Production process for both manufacturing industry and service industry can be classified into broad categories based on standardization of product or service. It can range from single project assignment like a building or bridge (manufacturing) to interior design (service) and mass production project like a car (manufacturing) to a fast-food joint (Services).

Process Design

A successful process design has to take into account the appropriateness of the process to overall organization objective. Process design requires a broad view of the whole organization and should not have a myopic outlook. And the process should deliver customer value with constant involvement of the management at various stages.

In order to achieve a good process design, effective process strategy is required, which deals with a singular line items required to manufacture the end product. Effective process strategy deals with raw material procurement, customer participation, technology investment, etc.

Over a period of time process design has undergone change and new concepts like Flexible Manufacturing Systems have been developed, which delivers efficient and effective production design and analysis.

Integrated Product and Process Development - Meaning, Advantages and Key Factors

Introduction

Objective of any organization is to provide customer satisfaction by building product and services, which not only satisfy needs and want but also create value for them.

This requires product design based on the customer feedback and production process which not only minimizes cost but also provides a competitive advantage. However, most organizations tend to follow conventional production method and process.

However, in the global age of new technology and competition organization have to re-invent the way they cater to needs of customer, focus on specialization and customization is ever increasing. Given this scenario it is imperative for the organization to integrate technology and innovation within the framework of integrated product and process development.

Integrated Product and Process Development(IPPD)

Integrated product and process development combines the product design processes along with the process design process to create a new standard for producing competitive and high-quality products.

Integration of new technologies and methods provide a complete new dimension to product design process. This process starts with defining of the requirements of products based on the customer feedback while considering the design layout and other constraints. Once the finer details are finalized, they are fed into CAD models where extensive testing and modeling are done to get the best product.

With integration of production method and technology with product design, it is natural for integration of product design and process design. Therefore, integrated product and process development can be defined as a process starting from product idea to development of final product through modern technology and process management practices while minimizing cost and maximizing efficiency.

Advantages of Integrated Product and Process Development (IPPD)

Organization stands to benefit greatly from the implementation of IPPD. Some of the advantages are as follows:

- Using modern technologies and implement logical steps in production design, the actual production is likely to come down, thereby reducing product delivery time.
- Through optimum usage of resources and using efficient process, organizations are able to minimize cost of production thus improving profitability of the organization.
- Since extensive uses of CAD model are employed chances are of product or design failure are greatly reduced thus reducing risk for organization.
- As the focus is solely in delivering value to customer, quality is paramount importance and achieved through technology and methods.

Key Factors for IPPD

There are certain factors, which can vastly improve IPPD. These factors are as follows:

- IPPD success is greatly dependent on agreement on the end objective which is the successful address to customer requirements. All the stakeholders and management should be aligned to the single objective.

- Since this is a scientific approach, its success dependent on building up of plan, implementation of plan and constant review of the implemented plan.

- With implementation of modern methods and technology comes usage of modern tools and systems. This tools, and systems need to be integrated within the organization framework.

- Skilled manpower is another essential; therefore, organization need to make investment in human capital.

Customer is the focal point of IPPD. Therefore, constant feedback from them is essential for IPPD to be a success.

Therefore, IPPD is approach design to address all the concern of modern organization in the globalized world.

Facility Location - Factors Influencing the Location

Facility Location is the right location for the manufacturing facility, it will have sufficient access to the customers, workers, transportation, etc. For commercial success, and competitive advantage following are the critical factors:

Overall objective of an organization is to satisfy and delight customers with its product and services. Therefore, for an organization it becomes important to have strategy formulated around its manufacturing unit. A manufacturing unit is the place where all inputs such as raw material, equipment, skilled labors, etc. come together and manufacture products for customers. One of the most critical factors determining the success of the manufacturing unit is the location.

Facility location determination is a business critical strategic decision. There are several factors, which determine the location of facility among them competition, cost and corresponding associated effects. Facility location is a scientific process utilizing various techniques.

Location Selection Factors

For a company which operates in a global environment; cost, available infrastructure, labor skill, government policies and environment are very important factors. A right location provides adequate access to customers, skilled labors, transportation, etc. A right location ensures success of the organization in current global competitive environment.

Industrialization

A geographic area becomes a focal point for various facility locations based on many factors, parameters and issues. These factors are can be divided into primary factors and secondary factors. A primary factor which leads to industrialization of a particular area for particular manufacturing of products is material, labor and presence of similar manufacturing facilities. Secondary factors are available of credit finance, communication infrastructure and insurance.

Errors in Location Selection

Facility location is critical for business continuity and success of the organization. So it is important to avoid mistakes while making selection for a location. Errors in selection can be divided into two broad categories behavioral and non-behavioral. Behavioral errors are decision made by executives of the company where personal factors are considered before success of location, for example, movement of personal establishment from hometown to new location facility. Non-behavioral errors include lack of proper investigative practice and analysis, ignoring critical factors and characteristics of the industry.

Location Strategy

The goal of an organization is customer delight for that it needs access to the customers at minimum possible cost. This is achieved by developing location strategy. Location strategy helps the company in determining product offering, market, demand forecast in different markets, best location to access customers and best manufacturing and service location.

Factors Influencing Facility Location

If the organization can configure the right location for the manufacturing facility, it will have sufficient access to the customers, workers, transportation, etc. For commercial success, and competitive advantage following are the critical factors:

Customer Proximity: Facility locations are selected closer to the customer as to reduce transportation cost and decrease time in reaching the customer.

Business Area: Presence of other similar manufacturing units around makes business area conducive for facility establishment.

Availability of Skill Labor: Education, experience and skill of available labor are another important, which determines facility location.

Free Trade Zone/Agreement: Free-trade zones promote the establishment of manufacturing facility by providing incentives in custom duties and levies. On another hand free trade agreement is among countries providing an incentive to establish business, in particular, country.

Suppliers: Continuous and quality supply of the raw materials is another critical factor in determining the location of manufacturing facility.

Environmental Policy: In current globalized world pollution, control is very important, therefore understanding of environmental policy for the facility location is another critical factor.

Facility Layout - Objectives, Design and Factors Affecting the Layout

Introduction

For an organization to have an effective and efficient manufacturing unit, it is important that special attention is given to facility layout. Facility layout is an arrangement of different aspects of manufacturing in an appropriate manner as to achieve desired production results. Facility layout considers available space, final product, safety of users and facility and convenience of operations.

An effective facility layout ensures that there is a smooth and steady flow of production material, equipment and manpower at minimum cost. Facility layout looks at physical allocation of space for economic activity in the plant. Therefore, main objective of the facility layout planning is to design effective workflow as to make equipment and workers more productive.

Facility Layout Objective

A model facility layout should be able to provide an ideal relationship between raw material, equipment, manpower and final product at minimal cost under safe and comfortable environment. An efficient and effective facility layout can cover following objectives:

- To provide optimum space to organize equipment and facilitate movement of goods and to create safe and comfortable work environment.
- To promote order in production towards a single objective
- To reduce movement of workers, raw material and equipment
- To promote safety of plant as well as its workers
- To facilitate extension or change in the layout to accommodate new product line or technology upgradation
- To increase production capacity of the organization

An organization can achieve the above-mentioned objective by ensuring the following:

- Better training of the workers and supervisors.
- Creating awareness about of health hazard and safety standards
- Optimum utilization of workforce and equipment

- Encouraging empowerment and reducing administrative and other indirect work

Factors affecting Facility Layout

Facility layout designing and implementation is influenced by various factors. These factors vary from industry to industry but influence facility layout. These factors are as follows:

- The design of the facility layout should consider overall objectives set by the organization.
- Optimum space needs to be allocated for process and technology.
- A proper safety measure as to avoid mishaps.
- Overall management policies and future direction of the organization

Design of Facility Layout

Principles which drive design of the facility layout need to take into the consideration objective of facility layout, factors influencing facility layout and constraints of facility layout. These principles are as follows:

- **Flexibility:** Facility layout should provide flexibility for expansion or modification.

- **Space Utilization:** Optimum space utilization reduces the time in material and people movement and promotes safety.
- **Capital:** Capital investment should be minimal when finalizing different models of facility layout.

Design Layout Techniques

There are three techniques of design layout, and they are as follows:

1. **Two or Three Dimensional Templates:** This technique utilizes development of a scaled-down model based on approved drawings.
2. **Sequence Analysis:** This technique utilizes computer technology in designing the facility layout by sequencing out all activities and then arranging them in circular or in a straight line.
3. **Line Balancing:** This kind of technique is used for assembly line.

Types of Facility Layout

There are six types of facility layout, and they are as follows:

- Line Layout

- Functional Layout

- Fixed Position Layout

- Cellular Technology Layout

- Combined Layout, and

- Computerized Relative Allocation of Facility Technique

- Demand Forecasting - Objectives, Classification and Characteristics of a Good Forecast

Forecasting

For an organization to provide customer delight it is important that organization can understand what customer wants and how much does they want. If an organization can gauge future demand that manufacturing plan becomes simpler and cost effective.

The process of analyzing and understanding current and past information to understand the future patterns through a scientific and systemic approach is called forecasting. And the process of estimating the future demand of product in terms of a unit or monetary value is referred to as demand forecasting.

The purpose of forecasting is to help the organization manage the present as to prepare for the future by examining the most probable future demand pattern. However, forecasting has its constraint for example we cannot estimate a pattern for technologies and product where there are no existing pattern or data.

Business Forecasting Objective

The very objective of business forecasting is to be accurate as possible, so that planning of resources can be done in a very economical manner and therefore, propagate optimum utilization of resources. Business forecasting helps in establishing relationship among many variables, which go into manufacturing of the product. Each forecast situation must be analyzed independently along with forecasting method.

Classification of Business Forecasting

Business forecasting has many dimensions and varieties depending upon the utility and application. The three basic forms are as follows:

Economic Forecasting: these forecasting are related to the broader macro-economic and micro-economic factors prevailing in the current business environment. It includes forecasting of inflation rate, interest rate, GDP, etc. at the macro level and working of particular industry at the micro level.

Demand Forecast: organization conduct analysis on its pre-existing database or conduct market survey as to understand and predict future demands. Operational planning is done based on demand forecasting.

Technology Forecast: this type of forecast is used to forecast future technology up gradation.

Timeline of Business Forecasting

A forecast and its conclusion are valid within specific time frame or horizon. These time horizons are categorized as follows:

Long Term Forecast: This type of forecast is made for a time frame of more than three years. These types of forecast are utilized for long-term strategic planning in terms of capacity planning, expansion planning, etc.

Mid-Term Forecast: This type of forecast is made for a time frame from three months to three years. These types of forecasts are utilized production and layout planning, sales and marketing planning, cash budget planning and capital budget planning.

Short Term Forecast: This type of forecast is made of a time frame from one day to three months. These types of forecasts are utilized for day to day production planning, inventory planning, workforce application planning, etc.

Characteristics of Good Forecast

A good forecast is should provide sufficient time with a fair degree of accuracy and reliability to prepare for future demand. A good forecast should be simple to understand and provide information relevant to production (e.g. units, etc.)

Forecasting Methods

Forecasting is divided into two broad categories, techniques and routes. Techniques are further classified into quantitative techniques and qualitative techniques. Quantitative techniques comprise of time series method, regression analysis, etc., where as qualitative methods comprise of Delphi method, expert judgment.

Routes forecasting consist of top-down route and bottom-up route.

Capacity Planning

The production system design planning considers input requirements, conversion process and output. After considering the forecast and long-term planning organization should undertake capacity planning.

Capacity is defined as the ability to achieve, store or produce. For an organization, capacity would be the ability of a given system to produce output within the specific time period. In operations, management capacity is referred as an amount of the input resources available to produce relative output over period of time.

In general, terms capacity is referred as maximum production capacity, which can be attained within a normal working schedule.

Capacity planning is essential to be determining optimum utilization of resource and plays an important role decision-making process, for example, extension of existing operations, modification to product lines, starting new products, etc.

Strategic Capacity Planning

A technique used to identify and measure overall capacity of production is referred to as strategic capacity planning. Strategic capacity planning is utilized for capital intensive resource like plant, machinery, labor, etc.

Strategic capacity planning is essential as it helps the organization in meeting the future requirements of the organization. Planning ensures that operating cost are maintained at a minimum possible level without affecting the quality. It ensures the organization remain competitive and can achieve the long-term growth plan.

Capacity Planning Classification

Capacity planning based on the timeline is classified into three main categories long range, medium range and short range.

Long Term Capacity: Long range capacity of an organization is dependent on various other capacities like design capacity, production capacity, sustainable capacity and effective capacity. Design capacity is the maximum output possible as indicated by equipment manufacturer under ideal working condition.

Production capacity is the maximum output possible from equipment under normal working condition or day.

Sustainable capacity is the maximum production level achievable in realistic work condition and considering normal machine breakdown, maintenance, etc.

Effective capacity is the optimum production level under pre-defined job and work-schedules, normal machine breakdown, maintenance, etc.

Medium Term Capacity: The strategic capacity planning undertaken by organization for 2 to 3 years of a time frame is referred to as medium term capacity planning.

Short Term Capacity: The strategic planning undertaken by organization for a daily weekly or quarterly time frame is referred to as short term capacity planning.

Goal of Capacity Planning

The ultimate goal of capacity planning is to meet the current and future level of the requirement at a minimal wastage. The three types of capacity planning based on goal are lead capacity planning, lag strategy planning and match strategy planning.

Factors Affecting Capacity Planning

Effective capacity planning is dependent upon factors like production facility (layout, design, and location), product line or matrix, production technology, human capital (job design, compensation), operational structure (scheduling, quality assurance) and external structure (policy, safety regulations)

Forecasting v/s Capacity Planning

There would be a scenario where capacity planning done on a basis of forecasting may not exactly match. For example, there could be a scenario where demand is more than production capacity; in this situation, a company needs to fulfill its requirement by buying from outside. If demand is equal to production capacity; company is in a position to use its production capacity to the fullest. If the demand is less than the production capacity, company can choose to reduce the production or share it output with other manufacturers.

What is Aggregate Planning ? - Importance and its Strategies

Introduction

An organization can finalize its business plans on the recommendation of demand forecast. Once business plans are ready, an organization can do backward working from the final sales unit to raw materials required. Thus annual and quarterly plans are broken down into labor, raw material, working capital, etc. requirements over a medium-range period (6 months to 18 months). This process of working out production requirements for a medium range is called aggregate planning.

Factors Affecting Aggregate Planning

Aggregate planning is an operational activity critical to the organization as it looks to balance long-term strategic planning with short term production success. Following factors are critical before an aggregate planning process can actually start;

- A complete information is required about available production facility and raw materials.

- A solid demand forecast covering the medium-range period

- Financial planning surrounding the production cost which includes raw material, labor, inventory planning, etc.

- Organization policy around labor management, quality management, etc.

For aggregate planning to be a success, following inputs are required;

- An aggregate demand forecast for the relevant period

- Evaluation of all the available means to manage capacity planning like sub-contracting, outsourcing, etc.

- Existing operational status of workforce (number, skill set, etc.), inventory level and production efficiency

Aggregate planning will ensure that organization can plan for workforce level, inventory level and production rate in line with its strategic goal and objective.

Aggregate planning as an Operational Tool

Aggregate planning helps achieve balance between operation goal, financial goal and overall strategic objective of the organization. It serves as a platform to manage capacity and demand planning.

In a scenario where demand is not matching the capacity, an organization can try to balance both by pricing, promotion, order management and new demand creation.

In scenario where capacity is not matching demand, an organization can try to balance the both by various alternatives such as.

- Laying off/hiring excess/inadequate excess/inadequate excess/inadequate workforce until demand decrease/increase.
- Including overtime as part of scheduling there by creating additional capacity.
- Hiring a temporary workforce for a fix period or outsourcing activity to a sub-contrator.

Importance of Aggregate Planning

Aggregate planning plays an important part in achieving long-term objectives of the organization. Aggregate planning helps in:

- Achieving financial goals by reducing overall variable cost and improving the bottom line
- Maximum utilization of the available production facility
- Provide customer delight by matching demand and reducing wait time for customers
- Reduce investment in inventory stocking
- Able to meet scheduling goals there by creating a happy and satisfied work force

Aggregate Planning Strategies

There are three types of aggregate planning strategies available for organization to choose from. They are as follows.

1. Level Strategy

As the name suggests, level strategy looks to maintain a steady production rate and workforce level. In this strategy, organization requires a robust forecast demand as to increase or decrease production in anticipation of lower or higher customer demand. Advantage of level strategy is steady workforce. Disadvantage of level strategy is high inventory and increase back logs.

2. Chase Strategy

As the name suggests, chase strategy looks to dynamically match demand with production. Advantage of chase strategy is lower inventory levels and back logs. Disadvantage is lower productivity, quality and depressed work force.

3. Hybrid Strategy

As the name suggests, hybrid strategy looks to balance between level strategy and chase strategy.

Materials and Resource Requirement Planning

Introduction

Success of an operation department of any organization is dependent upon an efficient production plan. One of the key essential of a production plan is material and manufacturing planning system. Material requirement planning plays a pivotal role in assembly-line production. Material requirement planning is a system based approach, which organizes all required production material.

Material requirement planning is an information system for production planning based on inventory management. The basic components of material planning are:

- Material planning provides information that all the required raw material and products are available for production.

- Material planning ensures that inventory level are maintained at its minimum levels. But also ensures that material and product are available whenever production is scheduled, therefore, helping in matching demand and supply.

- Material planning provides information of production planning and scheduling but also provides information around dispatch and stocking.

Objective of Material Requirement Planning

Material requirement planning is processed which production planning and inventory control system, and its three objectives are as follows:

- Primary objective is to ensure that material and components are available for production, and final products are ready for dispatch.

- Another primary objective is not only to maintain minimum inventory but also ensure right quantity of material is available at the right time to produce right quantity of final products.

- Another primary objective is to ensure planning of all manufacturing processes, this scheduling of different job works as to minimize or remove any kind of idle time for machine and workers.

Advantages and Disadvantages of Material Resource Planning

As with every system based process, material resource planning also has its advantages and disadvantages, and they are as follows:

Advantages of Material Resource Planning

- It helps in maintain minimum inventory levels.
- With minimum inventory levels, material planning also reduces associated costs.
- Material tracking becomes easy and ensures that economic order quantity is achieved for all lot orders.
- Material planning smoothens capacity utilization and allocates correct time to products as per demand forecast.

Disadvantages of Material Resource Planning

- Material planning is highly dependent on inputs it receives from other systems or department. If input information is not correct than output for material planning will also be incorrect.
- Material planning requires maintenance of robust database with all information pertaining inventory

records, production schedule, etc. without which output again would be incorrect.

- Material planning system requires proper training for end users, as to get maximum out of the system.

- Material resource planning system requires substantial investment of time and capital.

Material Resource Planning - Inter dependency of Business Function

Material planning not only benefits operation department but is also beneficial to the other department of organization. They are as follows:

- Material planning is useful in determining cash flow requirement based on material requirements and final dispatch schedules.

- It helps procurement team in scheduling purchase of necessary material.

- It helps the sales team in determining delivery dates for final products.

Implementation of Material Resource Planning

Implementation and success of material resource planning dependent on following factors:

- Acceptability of by top management about advantages and benefits

- Proper training and participation of all workers and personnel

- Precision and accuracy of input data for accurate and reliable results

Production Planning and Control

Introduction

For efficient, effective and economical operation in a manufacturing unit of an organization, it is essential to integrate the production planning and control system. Production planning and subsequent production control follow adaption of product design and finalization of a production process.

Production planning and control address a fundamental problem of low productivity, inventory management and resource utilization.

Production planning is required for scheduling, dispatch, inspection, quality management, inventory management, supply management and equipment management. Production control ensures that production team can achieve required production target, optimum utilization of resources, quality management and cost savings.

Planning and control are an essential ingredient for success of an operation unit. The benefits of production planning and control are as follows:

- It ensures that optimum utilization of production capacity is achieved, by proper scheduling of the machine items which reduces the idle time as well as over use.

- It ensures that inventory level are maintained at optimum levels at all time, i.e. there is no over-stocking or under-stocking.

- It also ensures that production time is kept at optimum level and thereby increasing the turnover time.

- Since it overlooks all aspects of production, quality of final product is always maintained.

Production Planning

Production planning is one part of production planning and control dealing with basic concepts of what to produce, when to produce, how much to produce, etc. It involves taking a long-term view at overall production planning. Therefore, objectives of production planning are as follows:

- To ensure right quantity and quality of raw material, equipment, etc. are available during times of production.

- To ensure capacity utilization is in tune with forecast demand at all the time.

A well thought production planning ensures that overall production process is streamlined providing following benefits:

- Organization can deliver a product in a timely and regular manner.
- Supplier are informed will in advance for the requirement of raw materials.
- It reduces investment in inventory.
- It reduces overall production cost by driving in efficiency.

Production planning takes care of two basic strategies' product planning and process planning. Production planning is done at three different time dependent levels i.e. long-range planning dealing with facility planning, capital investment, location planning, etc.; medium-range planning deals with demand forecast and capacity planning and lastly short term planning dealing with day to day operations.

Production Control

Production control looks to utilize different type of control techniques to achieve optimum performance out of the production system as to achieve overall production planning targets. Therefore, objectives of production control are as follows:

- Regulate inventory management
- Organize the production schedules
- Optimum utilization of resources and production process

The advantages of robust production control are as follows:

- Ensure a smooth flow of all production processes
- Ensure production cost savings thereby improving the bottom line
- Control wastage of resources
- It maintains standard of quality through the production life cycle.

Production control cannot be same across all the organization. Production control is dependent upon the following factors:

- Nature of production(job oriented, service oriented, etc.)
- Nature of operation
- Size of operation

Production planning and control are essential for customer delight and overall success of an organization.

Operations Scheduling and Workplace Planning

Introduction

Scheduling and workplace planning is the final step in operation planning and design. Operation's scheduling and workplace planning is implemented during transformation of input to output. Scheduling deals with production of required quantity of product within the required time frame. Workplace planning deals with allocation of resources with priority to work job with first delivery date.

Operations Planning

Scheduling deals with both time allocations as well resource allocation for production of required quantity. Operations' planning is done as part of short term planning.

High level objective of operation's planning is to decide the best way of allocation of labor and equipment as to find balance between time and use of limited resources within the organization.

In modern age of competition and global market importance is given to Just In Time and the lean production concepts. This has led to importance of operation's scheduling. There are three important task performed by operations scheduling:

- Allocation of resources
- Workforce scheduling
- Production equipment scheduling

Operations' planning ensures that proper workflow is established by ensuring allocation of job on appropriate machines before the advent of production activities. Scheduling is production timetable highlighting sequence of job, timing and quantity for allocation of resources as to help an organization in cash flow planning. Therefore, there are three main objectives of production scheduling:

- Due importance to delivery date and avoiding delays in completion
- Reducing time of job on machines
- Proper utilization of work centers

Operation scheduling is arrived at base on the following principles.

- Ensure continuous job schedule
- End to end completion of job

- Remove the bottleneck
- Ensure feedback as to make adjustment
- Skill set of workforce
- Enhancement of product and process
- Scheduling helps in capacity planning as to reduce bottlenecks.
- Scheduling helps in streamlining order production based on due date.
- Scheduling helps in sequencing of various job works.

Scheduling is done with two approaches, and they are as follows:

- Forward scheduling is type of scheduling where the planner considers order received date as the starting point for forward planning of all the activities.
- Backward scheduling is type of scheduling where the planner considers the order delivery date as the starting point and does backward planning of all activities.

Workplace Planning

Workplace planning ensures optimum productivity by ensuring proper utilization of limited resources and priorities' job order at different work centers. Workforce control ensures that maximum output is achieved from machines, raw material and workforce. All production-related information is recorded as to establish input-output control as to achieve overall efficiency and optimum utilization of raw materials.

The main objectives of workforce planning and control are as follows:

- Priorities various job orders
- Record data related to process quantities
- Providing status of workplace orders to control panel
- Record output data to monitor capacity control
- Provide measurement of efficiency and productivity

Therefore operations scheduling and workplace planning play an pivotal role in success of an organization.

Waiting Line (Queue) Management

Introduction

The waiting line or queue management is a critical part of service industry. It deals with issue of treatment of customers in sense reduce wait time and improvement of service. Queue management deals with cases where the customer arrival is random; therefore, service rendered to them is also random.

A service organization can reduce cost and thus improve profitability by efficient queue management. A cost is associated with customer waiting in line and there is cost associated with adding new counters to reduce service time. Queue management looks to address this trade off and offer solutions to management.

Waiting Line Problems

Waiting in line is common phenomena in daily life, for example, banks have customers in line to get service of teller, cars queue up for re-filling, workers line up to access machine to complete their job. Therefore, management needs to work on formulae, which will reduce wait time and create delighted customers without incurring an additional cost. Generally, queue management problems are trade off's situation between cost of time spent in waiting v/s cost of additional capacity or machinery.

Finite and Infinite Population

In a waiting line scenario, there are cases of finite population of customers and infinite population of customers.

A finite population scenario considers a fixed or limited size of customers visiting the service counter. It also assumes that customer once served will leave the line thus reducing overall population of customers. However finite population model also considers a scenario where the customer after getting served will re-visit the service counter for re-service, leading to increase in finite population.

An infinite population theory looks at a scenario where subtractions and addition of customer do not impact overall workability of the model.

Queuing System

To solve problems related to queue management it is important to understand characteristics of the queue. Some common queue situations are waiting in line for service in super-market or banks, waiting for results from computer and waiting in line for bus or commuter rail. General premise of queue theory is that there are limited resources for a given population of customers and addition of a new service line will increase the cost aspect to the business. A typical queue system has the following:

Arrival Process: As the name suggests an arrival process look at different components of customer arrival. Customer arrival could in single, batch or bulk, arrival as distribution of time, arrival in finite population or infinite population.

Service Mechanism: this looks at available resources for customer service, queue structure to avail the service and preemption of service. Underlining assumption here is that service time of customers is independent of arrival to the queue.

Queue Characteristics: this looks at selection of customers from the queue for service. Generally, customer selection is through first come first served method, random or last in first out. As a result, customers leave if the queue is long, customer leave if they have waited too long or switch to faster serving queue.

Service Configuration

Another aspect of waiting line management is the service configuration. There are four types of service configuration, and they are as follows:

- Single Channel, Single Phase (e.g. ship yards and car wash)
- Single Channel, Multi Phase (e.g. bank tellers)
- Multi Channel, Single Phase (e.g. separate queue of man and women for single ticket window)
- Multi Channel, Multi Phase (e.g. Laundromat, where option of several washers and several dryers)

Inventory Management and Just In Time (JIT)

Introduction

Supply-chain management plays a pivotal role in ensuring goods, and services are delivered on time to customers. Within supply-chain management, inventory management plays a central role. Inventory involves various cost, investment, space management, etc. Also there are chances that stored inventory may get damaged or get stolen adding to extra cost to the company. Therefore, it is important to have a robust inventory management for an organization.

Inventory Holding

For an organization, it becomes important to hold inventory for the following reason:

- Inventory holding ensures that operation delay do not impact delivery to customers.
- It also ensures that company can meet spikes or fluctuation in product demand.
- It ensures that there is flexibility in production.
- It ensures that any delay by suppliers do not affect

working of the company.

Considering the above inventory holding objectives, next step for the company is to make inventory related decision. Inventory decision involves two major considerations, first is the order quantity of the raw material and second is timing for placing those orders.

Inventory Models

Inventory management is based upon two basic models i.e independent demand inventory model and dependent demand inventory model.

- Independent Demand Inventory Model talks about raw material demand which is dependent upon prevailing market conditions and is not correlated to any raw material currently used by the organization. Finished goods is an appropriate example for independent demand inventory model.
- Dependent Demand Inventory Model talks about raw material demand which are integral parts of production and form important part of material resource planning.

For example, demand for raw material can be established as the basis of demand of finished products.

Inventory Costs

There are three broad categories of cost associated with inventory; holding cost, ordering cost and set up cost.

- Holding costs are carrying cost associated with inventory over a period of time. They include insurance, warehousing, interest, extra head-count, etc.
- Ordering costs are cost associated with purchasing of raw material and receiving raw materials. They include forms, order processing, office maintenance supplies and staff associated with ordering.
- Set Up Cost are cost associated with installation of machine for production. They include clean- up cost, re-tooling cost and adjustment cost.

Inventory management ensures that organizations are able to minimize cost and maximize profit.

Just In Time (JIT)

Just In Time is set of strategic activities, which are formulated to achieve maximum production with minimal maintenance of inventory. JIT as philosophy is applicable to various types of organization but on implement side it is more relevant with manufacturing operations.

For JIT system to be successful, there are two critical elements, attitude of workers/management and practice.

Fundamentals of JIT

JIT is based on the following fundamentals:

- JIT manufacturing and ordering
- Elimination of waste
- Lean management
- Signal System (Kanban)
- Push-Pull System

With the above fundamentals in place, JIT delivers the following:

- Continuous improvement of production and order processing.
- Elimination of non-value added activities and procedures.
- Simplification and advancement of the existing systems.

- Creation of safety environment and ensuring total quality management.
- Creation crossed skilled workers.

Warehouse and Materials Management

Introduction

Purchase of raw materials is an integral part of any business, i.e. manufacturing organization or service organization. Purpose of raw material is to be converted into finished goods for selling, but after purchase and before selling, they need to keep in safety and good care. The timeframe of storage can be short period or longer depending upon nature and requirement of materials.

Any damage or theft to the materials is going to increase cost to the organization. So it becomes important for organization to have a robust and effective warehouse as well as material's management.

Scope of Warehouse Management

The place where raw material and/or finished goods are stored is referred to as warehouse or store. Generally, warehouse is structure or building design keeping in mind raw material and finished goods it is going to store. Therefore, warehouse management should be able to:

- Receive the purchase goods and entered upon the stock register.

- Inventory Accounting of raw material, work-in-progress or finished goods.

- Preservation of the inventory

- Ability to access goods whenever called upon.

- Appropriate record keeping through coding as to preserve goods and reduce obsolescence.

- Proper stocking of goods as ensure smooth handling.

If above objectives are met, warehouse management significantly increases the overall efficiency of the production and organization. A robust warehouse management would ensure that:

- A smooth flow of production

- Appropriate layout management to reduce material handling and equipment handling

- Reduce to wastage as well as spoilage

- Eliminate the possibility of theft and damage

- Ensure preservation of environment and reduce pollution.

- Encourage cost reduction and driving efficiency

Warehouse Design

Warehouse design is art in which goods and material can be stored as to reduce wastage, cost of carrying and increase safety. The various factors considered for warehouse design are as follows:

- Easy material handling including receipt, dispatch and storage.
- Easy supervision of materials as well as personnel
- Reduce and control obsolescence of the goods by following appropriate method.
- Optimum utilization of space

Storage Location

There are three general ways in which goods are stocked as to reduce material handling and increase prompt access. They are as follows:

- Fixed position in which specific area is located where designated goods are stored. If the designated goods are not there, that space will remain empty. Fixed position encourages easy and traceable access to the goods.

- Random Storage in which goods are stored where ever space is available. Here maximum utilization of the space is achieved.

- Categorized fixed location in which particular set of products are placed randomly in the allotted space.

Material Management

Material management is a sub-set of warehouse management dealing exclusively material which contribute the maximum to completion of the end product. The objectives of material management are as follows:

- Lower the price of the raw materials.

- Reduce the cost of production and ensure the smooth flow of production.

- Maintain quality of raw material as well as finished goods.

- Maintain good relation with the supplier as to ensure a smooth flow of raw materials.

- Continuous improvement of the skill set of the workers thereby increasing overall efficiency within the organization.

Material Handling - Principles, Operations and Equipment

Introduction

Raw materials form a critical part of manufacturing as well as service organization. In any organization, a considerable amount of material handling is done in one form or the other. This movement is either done manually or through an automated process. Throughout material, handling processes significant safety and health; challenges are presented to workers as well as management. Therefore, manual material handing is of prime concern for health and safety professional, and they must determine practical ways of reducing health risk to the workers.

Material Handling

Manual material handling ranges from movement of raw material, work in progress, finished goods, rejected, scraps, packing material, etc. These materials are of different shape and sizes as well as weight. Material handling is a systematic and scientific method of moving, packing and storing of material in appropriate and suitable location. The main objectives of material handling are as follows:

- It should be able determine appropriate distance to be covered.
- Facilitate the reduction in material damage as to improve quality.
- Reducing overall manufacturing time by designing efficient material movement
- Improve material flow control
- Creation and encouragement of safe and hazard-free work condition
- Improve productivity and efficiency
- Better utilization of time and equipment

It is critical for manufacturing organization to identify importance of material handling principle as the critical step in promoting the job improvement process. Manual material handling significantly increases health hazard for the workers in from lower back injuries.

In the current competitive and globalized environment, it is important to control cost and reduce time in material handling. An efficient material handling process promotes:

- Design of proper facility layout

- Promotes development of method which improves and simplifies the work process
- It improves overall production activity.
- Efficient material handling reduces total cost of production.

Principles of Material Handling

Material handling principles are as follows:

- **Orientation Principle:** It encourages study of all available system relationships before moving towards preliminary planning. The study includes looking at existing methods, problems, etc.
- **Planning Principle:** It establishes a plan which includes basic requirements, desirable alternates and planning for contingency.
- **Systems Principle:** It integrates handling and storage activities, which is cost effective into integrated system design.
- **Unit Load Principle:** Handle product in a unit load as large as possible
- **Space Utilization Principle:** Encourage effective utilization of all the space available

- **Standardization Principle:** It encourages standardization of handling methods and equipment.

- **Ergonomic Principle:** It recognizes human capabilities and limitation by design effective handling equipment.

- **Energy Principle:** It considers consumption of energy during material handling.

- **Ecology Principle:** It encourages minimum impact upon the environment during material handling.

- **Mechanization Principle:** It encourages mechanization of handling process wherever possible as to encourage efficiency.

- **Flexibility Principle:** Encourages of methods and equipment which are possible to utilize in all types of condition.

- **Simplification Principle:** Encourage simplification of methods and process by removing unnecessary movements

- **Gravity Principle:** Encourages usage of gravity principle in movement of goods.

- **Safety Principle:** Encourages provision for safe handling equipment according to safety rules and regulation

- **Computerization Principle:** Encourages of computerization of material handling and storage systems
- **System Flow Principle:** Encourages integration of data flow with physical material flow
- **Layout Principle:** Encourages preparation of operational sequence of all systems available
- **Cost Principle:** Encourages cost benefit analysis of all solutions available
- **Maintenance Principle:** Encourages preparation of plan for preventive maintenance and scheduled repairs
- **Obsolescence Principle:** Encourage preparation of equipment policy as to enjoy appropriate economic advantage.

Material handling operations are designed based upon principles as discussed above. Material handling equipment consists of cranes, conveyors and industrial trucks.

Maintenance Policy and Repair

Introduction

Plant and machinery in the initial days always perform to their fullest capacity but as time goes with regular wear and tear, this becomes increasingly difficult. If proper and regular maintenance is undertaken than production capacity can be maintained at a more or less same level. Maintenance also requires replacement decisions. Replacement is a substitution of existing fixed asset with a new asset, which may enhance features capable of performing similar function. The need for replacement may arise because of normal use, obsolescence, early service failure, destruction, etc.

Maintenance

Maintenance is defined as a process in which working condition of plant or machinery is maintained at the optimum level as to give maximum output. Maintenance is done through repair, partial replacement and total replacement. Following is the significance of the maintenance policy:

- Maintenance policy ensures that equipments are always in ready and reliable condition. This ensures company is able respond to any sudden change in demand.

- Maintenance policy ensures that equipments are always calibrated to provide good-quality products and competitive advantage. This ensures that there are no sudden and frequent breakdowns and reduce production of defective products.

- Maintenance policy ensures that there are no major breakdowns. This ensures there is no lose of inventory or market share for companies following JIT philosophy.

- Maintenance policy ensures that costs are always controlled.

- Maintenance policy is particularly important in capital-intensive industries.

If organizations are not able to implement an effective maintenance policy than it can result in the following results:

- Full capacity utilization may not be achieved.

- Increase in production cost as fixed labor cost cannot be reduced.

- Increase in maintenance cost as more spare parts are required.
- Reduction in product quality and increase in wastage.
- Safety of workers and operators in jeopardy.

Maintenance Management

Maintenance management is process where available resources are regulated in a manner that plant and machinery can perform at specific levels. Maintenance management involves planning, scheduling and execution of maintenance-related activities. The main objectives of the maintenance management are as follows:

- Minimum level of production loss and minimum incidence of breakdown.
- Minimum level of wastage.
- Optimum usage of maintenance equipment and personnel.
- Quality of product is improved.

Planning and Scheduling

The maintenance department is responsible with planning and scheduling of maintenance in line with the requirement and expectation of the organization. Planning and scheduling needs to ensure that business as usual is not disturbed.

The following are key points to plan maintenance:

- Identify the equipment for maintenance and technique for maintenance.
- Categorize maintenance into routine, priority and emergency.
- Plan maintenance considering cost, time, space etc
- Material planning for maintenance requirements.
- Budget time and money requirements.

The need to schedule maintenance can be best described as follows:

- To optimize usage of plant, machinery and tools.
- To optimize usage of manpower in maintenance.
- To ensure smooth production flow.

From above it can safely be concluded that it is very critical for company to have a robust and effective maintenance and repair policy.

Quality - A Tool for Achieving Excellence

Introduction

For an organization to be successful it is of paramount importance to exceed the customer expectations as to generate customer delight. One of the best ways of doing this is by providing quality products and services.

In technical language, quality means to a product adhering to the specifications. For customer probably meeting or exceeding the expectation could be quality.

Therefore, quality has different meaning to different people, for example, in automobile industry quality means cars with no defects and works smoothly. Quality involves meeting and exceeding of customer expectations. So to summarize quality is:

- Satisfying customer defined standards.
- Meet customer needs
- Meet or exceed customer expectations.
- Satisfy future needs and requirements of customers.

Quality Definitions

According to industry and users quality has many definitions some of them are as follows:

- Customer Oriented Industry: Meeting customer expectation
- Manufacturing Industry: Meeting technical specification and working with no defects
- Product Oriented Industry: Product has additional value compared to similar products available in the market.
- Value Oriented Industry: Product is perfect combination of features in the given price band.

Accordingly, Customers look at quality in different areas as follows:

- Airline Industry: On time, low cost, comfortable
- Railways: On time, low cost, secure and safe
- Postal Service: Accurate delivery and cost effective

Total Quality Management (TQM)

The two main objectives of Total Quality Management are 100% customer satisfaction and zero defects. TQM is a process beyond quality of product or services; it deals with the business philosophy of the organization. TQM propagates the concept of doing right things right and at first time itself. In TQM:

- Total means involvement of top management as well as workers
- Quality means meeting expectation of the customers
- Management means management of quality across the organization

The main focus of the total quality management is as follows:

- Involvement of all employees in the process
- Selection of suppliers
- Organization structure to support the process
- Maximum customer satisfaction
- Appropriate reward for quality improvement and suggestions

Considering above focus points, scope of TQM can be defined as follows:

- Organization should encourage building of culture promoting TQM.

- Organizational resources, including infrastructure should be dedicated in TQM.

- Top management decision and structure should support the TQM process.

- Proper training and environment should be created before implementation of TQM.

Total Quality Management gives a great importance to customers and suppliers. Here customers and supplier both can be internal as well external. The relationship of organization with customers as well supplier is critical in continuation of TQM. Therefore, it is important to understand customers and suppliers.

Principles of Total Quality Management

The main principles of Total Quality Management are as follows:

- TQM proactively works towards prevention of quality problems.

- TQM strives to achieve a state with zero defects or minimal defects.

- TQM aims at producing right quality products at the first instance itself.

- TQM pushes the concept that quality is not the responsibility of production department but of organization as a whole.

- TQM encourages continuous improvement of business and production process.

- TQM encourages award and recognition for worker's pro-actively working towards quality.

- TQM decisions are fully based by research and data.

- TQM should be always systematic and logical in the process.

Quality Control Techniques

Introduction

Quality of product and services determines success or failure of the organization. Consumers expect the company to maintain high-level of quality and consider it an important aspect of satisfaction. Quality management, therefore, becomes very important as far as any organization is concerned. Quality management can be accomplished through various quality control techniques. Quality assurance and quality control are objective oriented and can be achieved through statistical quality control.

Statistical quality control requires usage of acceptance sampling and process control techniques. Statistical quality control extensively uses chart to measure the acceptance level of the product samples. Objective is to ensure that products fall within pre-decided upper control and lower control limits. Any sample falling outside the limits is inspected further for corrective action.

Quality Control

The quality of product or service is ensuring if proper designing process is followed. This designing process needs to be backed by appropriate process design supported by a suitable technology which confirms to requirements of customers. Quality control ensures that defects and errors are prevented and finally removed from the process or product. Therefore, quality control should include; planning, designing, implementation, gaps identification and improvisation. If organization can implement a stringent quality control than following benefits are possible:

- Reducing product defects lead to less variable cost associated with labor and material.
- Reduction in wastage, scrap and pollution.
- Ability to produce quality products over longer period of time
- With quality maintenance needs for inspection reduces leading to decrease in maintenance cost
- Large pool of satisfied customers.
- Increase in employee motivation and awareness of quality.
- Increase in productivity and overall efficiency.

Above mentioned points are relevant not only for production stage but are equally important for input material, manufacturing process, delivery process, etc.

Statistical Quality Control

Quality control techniques require extensive usage of statistical methods. The advantages of the statistical analysis are as follows:

- Statistical Tools are automated and therefore, require less manual intervention, leading cost reduction
- Statistical tools work on a model thus are very useful where testing requires destruction of products.

Statistical Quality tools can broadly be classified into following categories:

- Acceptance sampling is an important part of quality control wherein quality of products is assessed post production.
- Statistical process control helps in confirming whether the current process is falling within pre-determined parameters.

Acceptance Sampling

Acceptance sampling is done on sample's post production to check for quality parameters as decided by the organization covering both attributes as well as variables. If the sample does not meet the required parameters of quality than that given lot is rejected, and further analysis is done to identify the source and rectify the defects. Acceptance sampling is done on the basis of inspection, which includes physical verification of color, size, shape, etc.

The major objectives of inspection are:

- To detect and prevent defects in products and process.
- To identify defected parts or product and prevent it from further consumption or usage.
- To highlight the product or process defect to appropriate authorities for necessary and corrective actions.

Scope of inspection covers input materials, finished material, plant, machinery etc.

To sustain quality of product and services it is important to have in place robust quality control techniques.

World Class Manufacturing

Introduction

Manufacturing has evolved considerably since the advent of industrial revolution. In current global and competitive age, it is very important for organization to have manufacturing practice which is lean, efficient, cost-effective and flexible.

World class manufacturing is a collection of concepts, which set standard for production and manufacturing for another organization to follow. Japanese manufacturing is credited with pioneer in concept of world-class manufacturing. World class manufacturing was introduced in the automobile, electronic and steel industry.

World class manufacturing is a process driven approach where various techniques and philosophy are used in one combination or other.

Some of the techniques are as follows:

- Make to order
- Streamlined Flow
- Smaller lot sizes

- Collection of parts
- Doing it right first time
- Cellular or group manufacturing
- Total preventive maintenance
- Quick replacement
- Zero Defects
- Just in Time
- Increased consistency
- Higher employee involvement
- Cross Functional Teams
- Multi-Skilled employees
- Visual Signaling
- Statistical process control

Idea of using above techniques is to focus on operational efficiency, reducing wastage and creating cost efficient organization. This leads to creation of high-productivity organization, which used concurrent production techniques rather than sequential production method.

World Class Manufacturers

World class manufacturers tend to implement best practices and also invent new practices as to stay above the rest in the manufacturing sector. The main parameters which determine world-class manufacturers are quality, cost effective, flexibility and innovation.

World class manufacturers implement robust control techniques but there are five steps, which will make the system efficient. These five steps are as follows:

- **Reduction of set up time and in tuning of machinery:** It is important that organizations are able to cut back time in setting up machinery and also tune machinery before production.
- **Cellular Manufacturing:** It is important that production processes are divided into according to its nature, with similar nature combined together.
- **Reduce WIP material:** It is normal tendency of manufacturing organization to maintain high levels of WIP material. Increased WIP leads to more cost and decreased WIP induces more focus on production and fast movement of goods.
- **Postpone product mutation:** For to achieve a higher degree of customization many changes are made to final product. However, it is important that mutation

conceived for the design stage implement only after final operation.

- Removal the trivial many and focus on vital few: It is important for organization to focus on production of products which are lined with forecast demand as to match customer expectation.

Principles of World Class Manufacturing

There are three main principles, which drive world-class manufacturing.

- Implementation of just in time and lean management leads to reduction in wastage thereby reduction in cost.
- Implementation of total quality management leads to reduction of defects and encourages zero tolerance towards defects.
- Implementation of total preventive maintenance leads to any stoppage of production through mechanical failure.

Aspects of World Class Manufacturing

The main aspects of the world-class manufacturing are as follows:

- Industrial culture area

- Market/client area
- Product development area
- Operations area
- E-Performance area